GRACE LEE BOGGS: GARDENS OF HOPE

Songju Ma Daemicke

illustrated by Lin

Albert Whitman & Company
Chicago, Illinois

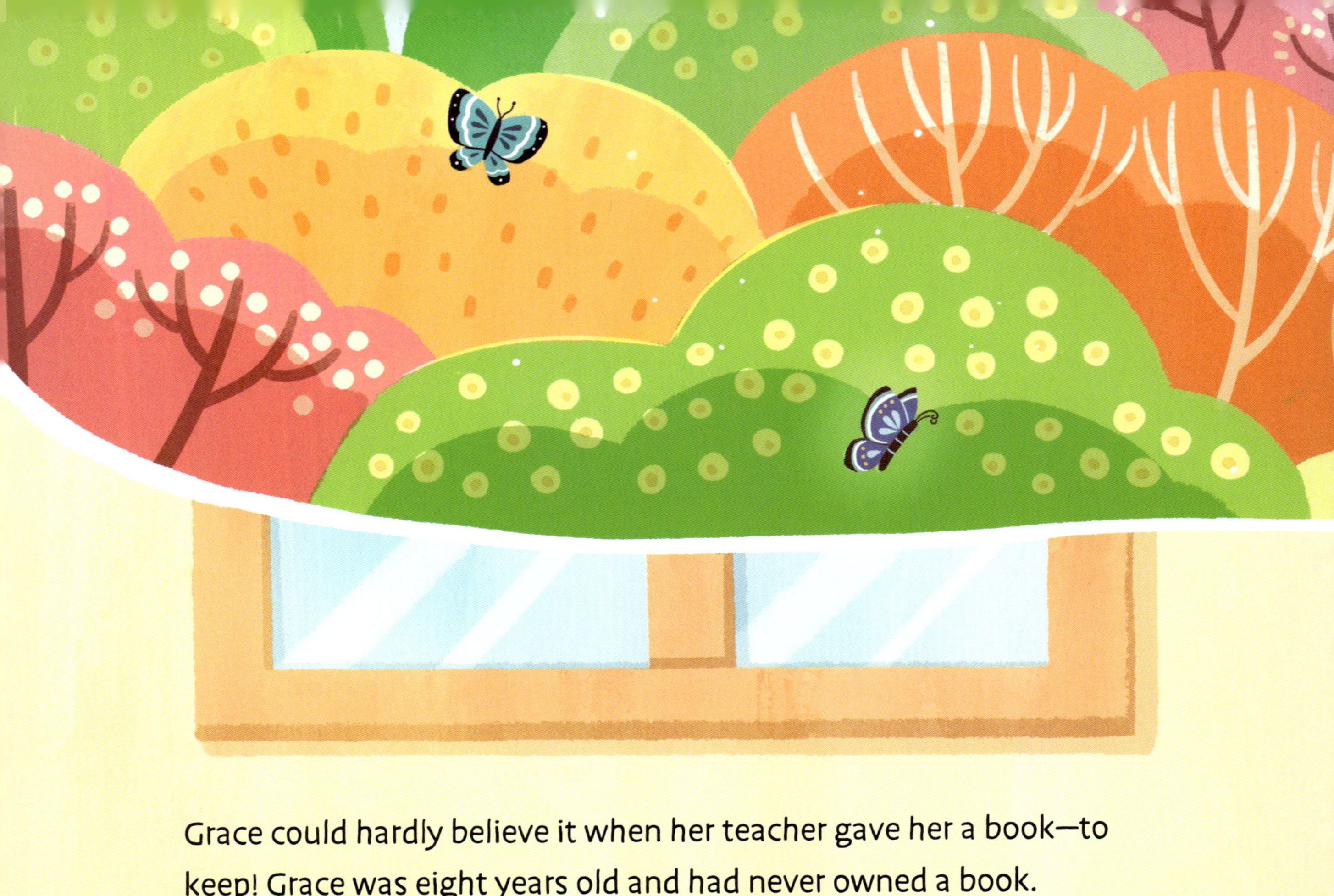

Grace could hardly believe it when her teacher gave her a book—to keep! Grace was eight years old and had never owned a book.

The Secret Garden, by Frances Hodgson Burnett, was about a lonely girl—just like Grace—who found an abandoned garden. The girl tended the garden with the help of her cousin and friend. As the garden bloomed, so did they.

Grace held the book against her chest and closed her eyes. She saw a garden full of flowers, hope, and possibilities.

I could grow a garden to help people heal.

But New York City, where Grace lived with her family, was crammed with gray sidewalks and tall buildings. Little room for gardens.

LEE
PLYMOUTH SHOPS
CHIN LEE

On the subway to school, people stared at Grace and her siblings as if they were aliens from outer space.

Stop looking at me like that, thought Grace. *Will Chinese people ever be treated the same?*

Grace studied hard, graduating college in 1940 with a PhD in philosophy. But no one in New York would hire her because she was Chinese. She felt trapped.

That fall, Grace found a job at the University of Chicago library, but all she could afford was a basement apartment. She had roommates...

Rats.

At a meeting of neighborhood tenants about rat-infested housing, Grace discovered the Workers Party, which fought for equal work rights. Most members were Black. Grace felt as if they were speaking for her.

She moved back to New York in 1942 to work for the Party and soon became a leader.

Because many autoworkers lived in Detroit, that's where Grace went in 1953. She reconnected with James "Jimmy" Boggs, a member of the Workers Party and a fellow activist whom she'd met in New York City a year before. They fell in love and got married.

Together, Grace and Jimmy organized marches and sit-ins, wrote books about Black activism, and hosted civil rights leader Malcolm X.

In 1963, Grace helped organize the Detroit Walk to Freedom march, led by Dr. Martin Luther King, Jr., who gave an early version of his "I Have a Dream" speech.

For decades, Grace fought tirelessly for civil, labor, women's, and environmental rights. During this time, Detroit remained a concrete jungle, just like New York City. Grace wondered if she would ever find her secret garden.

Robots and machines were replacing Detroit's autoworkers. Many lost their jobs and homes. Youth crime crushed the city. People despaired, but Grace and Jimmy saw an opportunity.

In 1992, they founded a program called Detroit Summer to nurture youth leadership. Grace and Jimmy brought children of all races together to focus on being healthy, kind, committed, and self-reliant—the kinds of young people who would create community change. Grace called them *"solutionaries,"* a word she heard a friend using and with which she identified.

There were not enough buses to get kids to the program, but the young people came up with a solution. In a church's youth space full of donated broken bikes, kids clinked and tinkered. The repaired bikes became their own clean-air transportation. Curious and neglected youth learned teamwork and new skills while gaining self-esteem and newfound freedom.

When residents complained about seven vacant lots on their block littered with old cars, tires, and trash, Grace checked them out. Seeing the lots, her eyes lit up. Grace felt as if she had found a rusty key to a mysterious gate.

Grace gathered young volunteers to rake, scour, and sweep. Together they dug, tilled, and sowed seeds. Soon, flowers blossomed. The volunteers added swings, slides, and sandboxes. Laughter and sweet floral scents filled the air. Grace's heart soared higher than the swings. At last! Grace had found her secret garden.

They planted vegetables, too. When the young people held their self-grown tomatoes and eggplants for the first time, they kissed them. Gardening taught Grace and her solutionaries how to relate to the earth. It also healed her wounds of past discrimination. Grace's secret garden gave her hope that these children would not have to go through what she had.

Grace was a gardener not only of plants but also of minds. Under a large maple tree, Grace talked with young people about art, the earth, and change, challenging them to turn ideas into action.

"We have to change ourselves in order to change the world. We are the leaders we are looking for."

Grace was planting a secret garden of possibility in young people, just like her teacher had once done when she gave Grace a book.

At the edge of their gardens, the young volunteers built and painted honeycomb billboards. They called them Detroit's Wall of Hope. The honeycombs represented the gardens and the young people who planted them. Their six-sided cells were stronger together than they were apart.

While plants in the garden thrived, the world outside remained barren and unfair. In 2003, the young volunteers created a Vincent Chin mural in Detroit's Chinatown as a social justice shout-out to life-threatening racism against Asians. WE WANT JUSTICE!

The gardens bloomed into a colorful canvas.
Flowers soothed wounded hearts.

Grace's seeds of hope spread, and gardens sprouted across Detroit: community gardens, school gardens, church gardens, hospital gardens...

Young people were growing not only flowers and vegetables but also their minds and souls.

Today, Grace's gardens continue to inspire new generations to make the world a healthier, kinder, and more just place for everyone.

AUTHOR'S NOTE

Grace Lee Boggs, born in 1915 to a restaurant-owner father and a homemaker mother who could not read Chinese or English, was a Chinese-American author and visionary activist. She was a pioneer in advocating for workers' rights, civil rights, women's rights, and the environment.

Grace had a unique vision for a twenty-first-century revolution: not a change of power but an evolution of humanity. People would live in harmony with each other and with nature, seeking a higher humanity instead of a higher standard of living.

Detroit Summer was a multicultural and intergenerational youth program founded by Grace and James Boggs in 1992. This award-winning program aimed to rebuild Detroit. It no longer exists in its original name but has evolved into many different and diverse organizations, including the James and Grace Lee Boggs Center, the James and Grace Lee Boggs School, the Detroit City of Hope, and the Detroit Asian Youth Project.

Grace was one of the only non-black leaders in the Black Power Movement. The FBI had a thick file describing her as "Afro-Chinese."

Some inspiring Grace Lee Boggs quotes:

"You cannot change any society unless you take responsibility for it, unless you see yourself as belonging to it and responsible for changing it."

"Real poverty is not just the lack of food, shelter, and clothing. Real poverty is the belief that the purpose of life is acquiring wealth and owning things. Real wealth is not the possession of property but the recognition that our deepest need, as human beings, is to keep developing our natural and acquired powers to relate to other human beings."

"You don't choose the times you live in, but you do choose who you want to be."

TIMELINE

1915 Grace Lee is born on June 27 in Providence, Rhode Island.

1924 Grace's family moves to New York.

1935 Grace graduates from Barnard College.

1940 Grace receives her PhD in philosophy from Bryn Mawr College in Pennsylvania.

1941 Grace joins the Workers Party.

1952 Grace meets James "Jimmy" Boggs in a Workers Party school in New York.

1953 Grace moves to Detroit to work on *Correspondence*, the Workers Party's magazine.

1954 Grace Lee marries James Boggs in Detroit, where they settle.

1963 Grace helps organize the Detroit Walk to Freedom event on June 23. The march, consisting of about 125,000 people, is led by Dr. Martin Luther King, Jr.

1964 Grace urges Malcolm X to run for the U. S. Senate. He declines.

1965 Grace and James found the Organization for Black Power (OFBP).

1970 The Boggses help found the Detroit Asian Political Alliance.

1992 The Boggses found Detroit Summer, a multicultural, intergenerational youth program.

1993 James Boggs dies.

1995 Friends and associates of the Boggses found the James and Grace Lee Boggs Center.

1998 Grace publishes her autobiography, *Living for Change.*

2013 The James and Grace Lee Boggs School opens in Detroit.

2015 Grace dies on October 5 at the age of 100.

I dedicate this book to Grace Lee Boggs
and all people who strive for positive social change.—SMD

Everyone should have the courage to change their lives.
Become a better self.—L

Library of Congress Cataloging-in-Publication data is on file with the publisher.

Illustrations by Lin
First published in the United States of America in 2025 by Albert Whitman & Company
ISBN 978-0-8075-3012-2 (hardcover)
ISBN 978-0-8075-3013-9 (ebook)

Printed in China
10 9 8 7 6 5 4 3 2 1 WKT 30 29 28 27 26 25

Design by Erin McMahon

For more information about Albert Whitman & Company,
visit our website at www.albertwhitman.com